Bond

Verbal Reasoning
10 Minute Tests

8–9 years

Frances Down

OXFORD
UNIVERSITY PRESS

TEST 1: Similars and Opposites

Test time: 0   5   10 minutes

Underline the pair of words most similar in meaning.

Example   come, go   <u>roam, wander</u>   fear, fare

1	book, word	story, tale	letter, pen
2	sight, vision	expect, delay	common, unusual
3	caught, loose	criminal, prison	free, release
4	cheese, biscuits	dish, bowl	bread, jam
5	stop, go	finish, halt	begin, end

Underline the two words, one from each group, which are most opposite in meaning.

Example   (dawn, <u>early</u>, wake)   (<u>late</u>, stop, sunrise)

6	(sensible, sense, every)	(feel, foolish, all)
7	(section, piece, war)	(peace, portion, argue)
8	(heavy, handsome, pale)	(pretty, eager, light)
9	(ripe, rise, steer)	(ready, guide, fall)
10	(mine, major, below)	(ours, minor, under)

Underline the word in the brackets closest in meaning to the word in capitals.

Example   UNHAPPY   (unkind   death   laughter   <u>sad</u>   friendly)

11	LIE	(down	sleep	bed	fib	truth)
12	CATCH	(escape	throw	capture	chase	ball)
13	WOMAN	(child	male	daughter	lady	man)
14	COMBINE	(harvest	divide	blend	separate	keep)
15	CHARGE	(attack	money	change	guard	coin)

Total

Rearrange the muddled letters in capitals to make a proper word. The answer will complete the sentence sensibly.

Example   A BEZAR is an animal with stripes.   _ZEBRA_

1   On November 5th, we are going to a IEOKRWFR display.   _____

2   Last Saturday and DYANUS, it rained all day.   _____

3   Over the summer, our lawn needed constant WMNIOG.   _____

4   Please be TUQEI and finish your work.   _____

5   Samantha painted a beautiful CTPIREU.   _____

Look at these groups of words.

GROUP A: COUNTIES   GROUP B: PLANETS

Choose the correct group for each of the following words. Write in the letter.

6   Kent   _____

7   Saturn   _____

8   Venus   _____

9   Durham   _____

10   Mars   _____

Underline the two words which are the odd ones out in the following groups of words.

Example   black   <u>king</u>   purple   green   <u>house</u>

11	difficult	hard	complex	simple	easy
12	horse	shoe	sandal	wood	boot
13	clock	watch	observe	look	sea
14	scarlet	brown	red	maroon	black
15	huge	immense	tiny	little	large

Total

Find the letter which will end the first word and start the second word.

Example   peac (_h_) ome

1   val   (____)   ach

2   lam   (____)   ook

3   hal   (____)   ish

4   jaz   (____)   one

5   car   (____)   cho

Add one letter to the word given in capital letters to make a new word. The meaning of the new word is given in the clue.

Example   PLAN   simple   _____plain_____

6   BUS   broken   _____

7   LOG   lengthy   _____

8   FAIL   delicate   _____

9   PINT   apply colour   _____

10   FLAT   opposite of sink   _____

Remove one letter from the word in capitals to leave a new word. The meaning of the new word is given in the clue.

Example   AUNT   an insect   _____ant_____

11   WIND   come first   _____

12   WHEAT   warmth   _____

13   CRANE   a walking stick   _____

14   BLEACH   seashore   _____

15   FLIGHT   not heavy   _____

Total

Test time: 0   5   10 minutes

Underline two words, one from each group, that go together to form a new word. The word in the first group always comes first.

Example   (hand, <u>green</u>, for)   (light, <u>house</u>, sure)

1 (fore, hand, right)   (head, fit, sore)   2 (off, chatter, back) (climb, box, on)

3 (best, high, kind)   (light, friend, nest)   4 (sock, wait, mush) (or, foot, room)

5 (way, up, stand)   (ran, set, at)

Complete the following sentences by selecting the most sensible word from each group of words given in the brackets. Underline the words selected.

Example   The (<u>children</u>, books, foxes) carried the (houses, <u>books</u>, steps) home from the (greengrocer, <u>library</u>, factory).

6   Every (hair, night, holiday) before you go to (bed, London, school) you must brush your (dogs, teeth, cars).

7   Danielle's (coat, hill, garden) is (blue, wild, steep) with (red, winding, frightened) buttons.

8   The (frightened, hungry, loud) (dog, girl, balloon) gnawed on his (thumb, bone, firework).

9   The (pretty, clean, rusty) hinge on the garden (flower, gate, post) (squeaked, spoke, cycled) loudly.

10   Yesterday it (shone, rained, flew) heavily and there were (tall, deep, sunny) puddles all over the (sky, playground, pond).

Choose the word or phrase that makes each sentence true.

Example   A LIBRARY always has (posters, carpets, <u>books</u>, DVDs, stairs).

11   A LAKE always has (ducks, a view, water, boats, fish).

12   A LAWN always has (grass, a path, chairs, daisies, a pond).

13   A DOG always has a (collar, master, dinner, face, bone).

14   A MAIN ROAD always has (cars, tarmac, yellow lines, puddles, pavements).

15   A DUSTBIN always has (rubbish, rats, sides, bottles, cardboard).

Total

Test time: 0   5   10 minutes

Find the three-letter word which can be added to the letters in capitals to make a new word. The new word will complete the sentence sensibly.

| Example | The cat sprang onto the MO. | USE |

1   The little boy cried when his BOON popped. _____

2   Neil likes bright colours like red and OGE. _____

3   Our hockey M is unbeaten so far this season. _____

4   Their GAR has a big lawn and a pond. _____

5   Our family likes to play on the SGS and slides in the park. _____

Write the four-letter word hidden at the end of one word and the beginning of the next word. The order of the letters may not be changed.

| Example | The children had bats and balls. | sand |

6   Please attach the labels to your jackets. _____

7   The match is hanging in the balance. _____

8   It is a good thing we are firm friends. _____

9   My sister makes me tidy my room. _____

10   Cutting my finger made me cry. _____

Underline the one word which **cannot be made** from the letters of the word in capital letters.

| Example | STATIONERY | stones | tyres | ration | <u>nation</u> | noisy |

11   CANDLES   snail   scale   dance   clean   lance

12   BASKETS   skate   state   tasks   steak   bakes

13   FEATHER   there   father   heart   thief   three

14   CLAMBER   crawl   cream   blame   brace   clear

15   TREACLE   crate   trace   trees   clear   react

Total

TEST 6: **Alphabetical Order and Substitution**

A B C D E F G H I J K L M N O P Q R S T U V W X Y Z

If these words were placed in alphabetical order, which word would come first? Underline the correct answer. The alphabet has been written out to help you.

1	brown	yellow	orange	white	purple
2	thigh	foot	chest	head	shoulder
3	July	August	September	October	November

In each line, underline the word which has its letters in alphabetical order.

4	petal	abbot	crime	tusks
5	salad	eight	flips	bossy
6	ghost	witch	moist	mouse
7	always	glory	stray	hover

Underline the word in each line which uses only letters from the first six letters of the alphabet.

8	baked	after	gladly	added
9	fable	guide	faced	caged
10	bead	ache	cats	fish

If a = 8, b = 2, c = 9 and d = 3, find the value of:

11 a + c + d =   _____

12 2b + 2d =   _____

13 3c – a =   _____

14 (c – a) + d =   _____

15 a + b + c + d =   _____

Total

Look at the first group of three words. The word in the middle has been made from the other two words. Complete the second group of three words in the same way, making a new word in the middle.

Example	PAIN	INTO	TOOK	ALSO	SOON	ONLY
1	BUSH	SHOP	OPEN	RUST	_____	IRON
2	CARS	CAPE	RIPE	PARK	_____	LESS
3	HORN	HOLE	LEAP	MOON	_____	REAL
4	CHIP	CAKE	WAKE	FLAN	_____	HIRE

Change the first word into the last word by changing one letter at a time and making a new, different word in the middle.

Example	CASE	CASH	LASH
5	TYRE	_____	FIRE
6	CASH	_____	CAKE
7	FORM	_____	FILM

Change the first word of the third pair in the same way as the other pairs to give a new word.

Example	bind, hind	bare, hare	but, hut
8	lamp, lump	sack, suck	care, _____
9	slow, glow	sale, gale	song, _____
10	first, fir	tinge, tin	hitch, _____
11	loaf, foal	team, meat	news, _____

Find the missing number by using the two numbers outside the brackets in the same way as the other sets of numbers.

Example	2 [8] 4	3 [18] 6	5 [25] 5
12	3 [4] 1	5 [7] 2	8 [__] 1
13	6 [5] 1	4 [1] 3	8 [__] 5
14	8 [11] 3	7 [12] 5	6 [__] 4
15	2 [6] 3	4 [8] 2	3 [__] 3

8

Total

Anne and Tom are wearing jeans.   Anne and Billie have pink tops.
Stan and Billie are wearing tracksuit bottoms. Stan and Tom have blue tops.

1   Who is wearing tracksuit bottoms and a pink top?   _____

2   Is Stan wearing a blue top and jeans?   _____

3   What is Anne wearing with her pink top?   _____

My bus should have arrived at 10:10. It is 15 minutes late.

4   What time is it now?   _____

The bus waited at the bus stop for 5 minutes before leaving, and the journey took 20 minutes.

5   What time did I arrive at my destination?   _____

The houses on one side of a street are even numbers from 2 to 20. On the other side they are odd numbers from 1 to 19. 1 is opposite 2, 3 is opposite 4 and so on. What number house is:

6 opposite 5? ___   **7** between 13 and 17? ___   **8** opposite 11? ___

Jake and Lewis own football boots.   Stuart and Lewis own rugby boots.
Jake and Pete have cricket boots.   Pete and Stuart have tennis shoes.

9   Who has tennis shoes and cricket boots?   _____

10   Who has rugby boots and football boots?   _____

A roasting joint weighs 2kg. It takes 45 minutes a kilogram to cook and must be done by 1pm. The potatoes will take 70 minutes and must be ready at the same time.

11–13 How long will the joint take to cook?   _____ hr _____ mins
          When should the food be put in the oven?   joint _____   potatoes _____

The day before yesterday was Wednesday. What is:

14   today? _____   **15**   the day after tomorrow? _____

Time for a break! Go to Puzzle Page 40 ▶   Total ☐

TEST 9: **Codes**

If the code for BEWARE is ZKPMHK, code and decode these words.

1 BEAR _____

2 RAW _____

3 BREW _____

4 ZMHK _____

5 PKMH _____

Here are four number codes.
7619 4613 1993 9674
Match them to the words below and then work out the missing code.

6 HAND _____

7 EACH _____

8 CANE _____

9 ACHE _____

10 NEED _____

Solve each question by working out the code.

11 If the code for TREAD is 67912, what is the code for DATE? _____

12 If the code for BEAST is FJODV, what is the code for BATS? _____

13 If the code for SLIME is BRPYX, what is the code for MILE? _____

14 If the code for PAINT is 35968, what is 3968? _____

15 If the code for THEME is $ + = * =, what is * = = $? _____

Total

Complete the following sentences in the best way by choosing one word from each set of brackets.

Example   Tall is to (tree, <u>short</u>, colour) as narrow is to (thin, white, <u>wide</u>).

1   Quick is to (slow, fast, clear) as dirty is to (close, far, clean).

2   Hat is to (scarf, head, warm) as glove is to (toes, hand, wool).

3   Three is to (four, seven, six) as five is to (ten, four, one).

4   Catch is to (ball, throw, draw) as rise is to (tall, follow, fall).

5   Go is to (depart, come, like) as small is to (little, round, far).

Fill in the missing letters and numbers.
The alphabet has been written out to help you.
A B C D E F G H I J K L M N O P Q R S T U V W X Y Z

Example   AB is to CD as PQ is to <u>RS</u>.

6   PN is to LJ as HF is to _____.

7   16a is to 14b as 12c is to _____.

8   ABD is to EFH as IJL is to _____.

9   K1L is to M2N as O3P is to _____.

Give the missing pairs of letters in the following sequences.
The alphabet has been written out to help you.
A B C D E F G H I J K L M N O P Q R S T U V W X Y Z

Example   CQ   DP   EQ   FP   GQ   <u>HP</u>

10	JK	LM	_____	PQ	RS	TU
11	FX	FW	_____	GU	GT	GS
12	_____	EG	IK	MO	QS	UW

Give the missing numbers in the following sequences.

Example   2   4   6   8   10   <u>12</u>

13	15	_____	23	27	31	35
14	21	18	15	_____	9	6
15	_____	4	8	16	32	64

Total

Rearrange the muddled letters in capitals to make a proper word. The answer will complete the sentence sensibly.

Example A BEZAR is an animal with stripes. _____ZEBRA_____

1 I have to go back to the STINTED for a filling. _____

2 David skilfully kicked the LLOBFATO. _____

3 In the MERUSM holidays we are going to France. _____

4 I like to watch the lambs GINYALP in the fields. _____

5 Let's cross the road on the NALIPEC crossing. _____

Underline the pair of words most opposite in meaning.

Example cup, mug   coffee, milk   <u>hot, cold</u>

6 frost, snow   fresh, ripe   salty, sweet

7 even, equal   flexible, rigid   dark, shade

8 ghost, train   fail, pass   speak, talk

9 sensible, foolish   crack, burst   rapid, fast

10 by, with   to, from   because, also

Solve each question by working out the code.

11 If the code for HOUSE is DRFPL, what is the code for SHOE? _____

12 If the code for SHAME is 70832, what is the code for MESH? _____

13 If the code for GREAT is DFMCV, what is the code for TEAR? _____

14 If the code for RIGHT is <^/#> , what is /<^> ? _____

15 If the code for BLAST is &*$^%, what is %$** ? _____

Total

Find the letter which will end the first word and start the second word.

Example   peac (_h_) ome

1   bro (___) and

2   mic (___) nds

3   pur (___) isk

4   kin (___) row

5   for (___) ish

Underline the number that completes each sequence.

6   40 is to 20 as 30 is to (20, 60, 15).

7   19 is to 17 as 35 is to (33, 37, 36).

8   5 is to 20 as 6 is to (10, 24, 18).

9   111 is to 222 as 333 is to (555, 444, 33).

10   11 is to 22 as 7 is to (14, 19, 77).

In each line, underline the word which has its letters in alphabetical order.

11 fever	doubt	most	roof
12 baby	pray	take	foot
13 bitten	know	farm	daisy
14 birth	whole	blast	adder
15 slab	raid	flop	dark

Total

TEST 13: **Mixed**

Find and underline the two words which need to change places for each sentence to make sense.

Example   She went to <u>letter</u> the <u>write</u>.

1   The little waves bobbed on the boat.

2   I am so sleepy that I feel really tired.

3   That woman is wearing not a coat.

4   There was a rumble of storm as the thunder broke.

5   Please help your meal with the mother.

Change one word so that the sentence makes sense. Underline the word you are taking out and write your new word on the line.

Example   I waited in line to buy a <u>book</u> to see the film.   _ticket_

6   Please close the window, as we need some fresh air in the room.   _____

7   As the road was icy and dangerous, Dad drove fast.   _____

8   The postman emptied the postbox and put the carrots in his sack.   _____

9   Hurry up or we will be early for the bus.   _____

10 In Spring, the days start to get shorter and warmer.   _____

Underline one word in the brackets which is the most opposite in meaning to the word in capitals.

Example   WIDE   (broad   vague   long   <u>narrow</u>   motorway)

11 COOL   (distant   frosty   icy   cold   warm)

12 DANGER   (safety   risk   peril   accident   road)

13 CLIMB   (ascend   mountain   descend   ladder   stairs)

14 EXTREME   (slight   great   serious   sports   maximum)

15 DEPART   (appear   go   depend   arrive   exceed)

Total [   ]

Test time: 0   5   10 minutes

Remove one letter from the word in capitals to leave a new word. The meaning of the new word is given in the clue.

	Example	AUNT	an insect	_ant_
1	WITCH		accompanying	_____
2	STABLE		not fresh	_____
3	SOFTEN		many times	_____
4	HARMFUL		amount you can carry	_____
5	MOTHER		alternative	_____

Find the four-letter word hidden at the end of one word and the beginning of the next word. The order of the letters may not be changed.

	Example	The children had bat<u>s and</u> balls.	_sand_
6		Please close the middle window.	_____
7		The baby monkey scampered up the tree.	_____
8		Kittens can be quite playful.	_____
9		A little after four o'clock, he left.	_____
10		Wendy and Sarah are coming as well.	_____

If the code for TRACTOR is WPFZWBP, what are the codes for the following words?

11	CART	_____
12	ROAR	_____
13	TACT	_____

Using the same code, decode:

14	ZBFW	_____
15	WPBW	_____

Total

Rearrange the muddled words in capital letters so that each sentence makes sense.

Example   There are sixty SNODCES __seconds__ in a UTMINE __minute__.

1–3 I am GIVANS _____ my TCPOKE _____ money to buy

a new CYLBCEI _____ .

4–5 Don't CHOUT _____ that dog; it may TIEB _____.

Read the school timetable, and then work out how many minutes each of the following activities takes.

Assembly   9:00
Maths   9:20
English   10:00
Reading   10:45
Break   11:00

6   Assembly   _____ minutes   **7**   Maths   _____ minutes

8   English   _____ minutes   **9**   Reading _____ minutes

I have 50p more than my sister, who has 80p less than my brother.
My brother has £5.50.

10   How much does my sister have?   _____

11   How much do I have?   _____

Underline two words, one from each group, that go together to form a new word. The word in the first group always comes first.

Example   (hand, green, for)   (light, house, sure)

12   (inter, ball, post)   (erupt, track, net)

13   (rain, suit, put)   (able, box, thing)

14   (sail, wasp, climb)   (or, up, bee)

15   (hard, my, be)   (time, bed, hind)

Total

Underline the two words, one from each group, which are the most opposite in meaning.

Example   (dawn, <u>early</u>, wake)   (<u>late</u>, stop, sunrise)

1   (still, cold, wet)   (chilly, quiet, dry)

2   (hard, cap, pillow)   (soft, hat, bed)

3   (change, shiny, coin)   (money, dull, safe)

4   (circle, add, multiply)   (line, number, divide)

5   (save, find, hide)   (conceal, place, protect)

Look at these groups of words.
Group A: MALE   Group B: FEMALE
Choose the correct group for each of the following words. Write in the letter.

6   girl   _____

7   bull   _____

8   uncle   _____

9   matron   _____

10 father   _____

Give the missing groups of letters and numbers in the following sequences.
The alphabet has been written out to help you.

ABCDEFGHIJKLMNOPQRSTUVWXYZ

Example	CQ	DP	EQ	FP	GQ	<u>HP</u>
11	ZY	XW	VU	TS	____	PO
12	____	bN	cM	dL	eK	fJ
13	4H	7G	4F	7E	4D	____
14	2X	4W	____	8U	10T	12S
15	QR	____	QT	QU	QV	QW

Time for a break! Go to Puzzle Page 40 ▶   Total [   ]

If a = 2, b = 5, c = 10, d = 4 and e = 3, find the value of the following calculations. Write the answer as a letter.

1 2a + 2e = _____

2 de − c = _____

3 bc − cd = _____

4 5b − 2c = _____

5 (b + d + e) − c = _____

Fill in the crosswords so that all the given words are included.
You have been given one letter as a clue in each crossword.

6 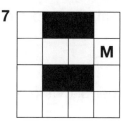   **7**   **8** 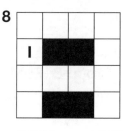   **9**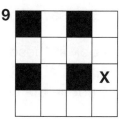

PARK   KING   SMUG   ATOM   STEP   NICE   FISH   THAT
PEEL   LUNG   TART   TANG   PINK   PASS   WINE   NEXT

Complete the following sentences by selecting the most sensible word from each group of words given in the brackets. Underline the words selected.

Example   The (<u>children</u>, books, foxes) carried the (houses, <u>books</u>, steps) home from the (greengrocer, <u>library</u>, factory).

10   The (green, tiny, clean) (mouse, house, stone) scampered through the (happy, tall, metal) grass.

11   Dragons are said to have (short, scaly, slow) skin, a long (list, tail, step) and to (breathe, eat, climb) fire.

12   Neeta put (in, away, up) her (elephants, books, rocks) and went (on, out, by) for break.

13   If we (eat, walk, beat) over the common, we will get to the (swings, pencil, picture) where we can (play, fight, snow).

14   For (lunch, bucket, lessons) we had (seaside, sausages, paper), chips and (traffic, salad, rulers).

15   The (imaginary, happy, tattered) (book, scarecrow, postcard) frightened the birds away from the (library, fridge, field).

Total

TEST 18: **Mixed**

Fill in the missing numbers and letters in the following sequences.

Example	2	4	6	8	10	_12_
1	15	18	____	24	27	30
2	5	10	20	40	____	160
3	6.5	7.0	7.5	8.0	____	9.0
4	1J1	2K2	3L3	____	5N5	6O6
5	5	6	8	11	15	____

Add one letter to the word given in capital letters to make a new word. The meaning of the new word is given in the clue.

Example	PLAN	simple	_plain_
6	ALL	tumble	_____
7	PICK	stab with a pin	_____
8	OUR	tip out	_____
9	STEAM	a little river	_____
10	PAY	worship	_____

If these words were placed in alphabetical order, which word would come last? Underline the word.

11	planet	space	rocket	moon	world
12	rabbit	horse	cat	dog	gerbil
13	traffic	tunnels	timber	thunder	tonsils
14	Friday	France	French	Frank	Freida
15	classical	claret	clarity	clarify	clarinet

Total

Rearrange the muddled words in capital letters so that each sentence makes sense.

Example   There are sixty SNODCES _seconds_ in a UTMINE _minute_.

1–2   It is time to put on your STOAC _____ and go DEOTUIS

_____ to play.

3–5   To reach the shops, you must turn GITRH _____ and walk

ASTIRTHG _____ down the ETREST _____ to the end.

Complete the following sentences in the best way by choosing one word from each set of brackets.

Example   Tall is to (tree, <u>short</u>, colour) as narrow is to (thin, white, <u>wide</u>).

6   Quick is to (slow, fast, yellow) as high is to (hill, low, green).

7   Pick is to (fruit, shovel, choose) as climb is to (descend, rise, steep).

8   Smooth is to (soft, skin, rough) as calm is to (boat, sunny, stormy).

9   Monday is to (yesterday, Tuesday, March) as Saturday is to (weekend, holiday, Sunday).

10   Paw is to (dog, toe, claw) as hoof is to (horse, shoe, kick).

These words have been written in code but the codes are not under the correct words. Find the correct code for each word.

STOP	POST	PORT	TRIP
7931	1657	5761	1697

11   STOP   _____

12   POST   _____

13   PORT   _____

14   TRIP   _____

Using the same code, decode:

15   51697   _____

Total

Underline one word in the brackets which is the most opposite in meaning to the word in capitals.

Example	WIDE	(broad	vague	long	<u>narrow</u>	motorway)
1	DISPLAY	(hide	show	present	wall	picture)
2	MERRY	(joyful	Christmas	gloomy	jolly	full)
3	PRESENT	(gift	wrap	here	absent	leave)
4	SECURE	(sound	safe	locked	guard	unsafe)
5	STRIPED	(patterned	plain	marked	pyjamas	tie)

Find the three-letter word which can be added to the letters in capitals to make a new word. The new word will complete the sentence sensibly.

Example   The cat sprang onto the MO.   <u>USE</u>

6   The wind blew the SUNFLRS over in her garden.   _____

7   Take your muddy boots off before you tread on the CAR.   _____

8   After school, our CHER marks our books.   _____

9   The fairy godmother waved her magic W.   _____

10   His THBRUSH and toothpaste are on the shelf.   _____

Choose the word or phrase that makes each sentence true.

Example   A LIBRARY always has (posters, carpets, <u>books</u>, DVDs, stairs).

11   A DOG always has a (dinner, collar, nose, bone, lead).

12   A ROOM always has (a carpet, furniture, pictures, walls, a fire).

13   A WOOD always has (trees, leaves, squirrels, paths, grass).

14   A BOTTLE always has (glass, milk, wine, sides, a straw).

15   A SHOE always has (a sole, laces, polish, an owner, a sock).

Total

Change the first word of the third pair in the same way as the other pairs to give a new word.

| Example | bind, hind | bare, hare | but, ___hut___ |

1	time, tame	wish, wash	stiff, _____
2	flame, fame	crane, cane	plain, _____
3	plug, gulp	doom, mood	dial, _____
4	bite, white	binge, whinge	bat, _____
5	meal, male	veal, vale	steal, _____

Underline the two words which are the odd ones out in the following groups of words.

| Example | black | <u>king</u> | purple | green | <u>house</u> |

6	foal	calf	beetle	duckling	wasp
7	many	some	lots	numerous	few
8	sum	add	metre	subtract	divide
9	line	talk	chat	row	discuss
10	anger	happy	rage	fury	laugh

Give the missing groups of letters and numbers in the following sequences. The alphabet has been written out to help you.

A B C D E F G H I J K L M N O P Q R S T U V W X Y Z

| Example | CQ | DP | EQ | FP | GQ | ___HP___ |

11	NM	LK	JI	____	FE	DC
12	OPA	QRA	STA	UVA	WXA	____
13	ab12	cd23	____	gh45	ij56	kl67
14	9OP	8QR	9ST	8UV	____	8YZ
15	ABB	____	ADD	AEE	AFF	AGG

Total

Find a word that can be put in front of each of the following words to make new, compound words.

Example	cast	fall	ward	pour	_down_

1	writing	cuff	some	shake	_____
2	surfing	swept	mill	screen	_____
3	sheet	shop	man	out	_____
4	scotch	fly	fingers	cup	_____
5	land	light	way	brow	_____

From the information below, work out which flavours of chocolates are in each of the spaces in the chocolate box.

TOP

NOUGAT	A	B
C	TOFFEE	D
E	F	COFFEE CUP

BOTTOM

The Nut Cluster is next to the Strawberry Delight but directly below the Chocolate Almond.

The Chocolate Log is closer to the top than the Nut Cluster but directly below the Tangerine Surprise, which is next to the Caramel Melt.

6	Nut Cluster	_____	7	Strawberry Delight	_____
8	Chocolate Almond	_____	9	Chocolate Log	_____
10	Tangerine Surprise	_____	11	Caramel Melt	_____

Fill in the crosswords so that all the given words are included. You have been given one letter as a clue in each crossword.

12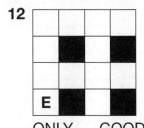

ONLY   GOOD
GAME   MALE

13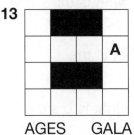

AGES   GALA
SAFE   HAZE

14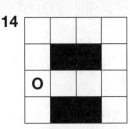

HUSH   BATH
OWLS   BOOK

15

JUMP   TURN
ZULU   SNIP

Total

Find and underline the two words which need to change places for each sentence to make sense.

Example She went to <u>letter</u> the <u>write</u>.

1 Come in quietly as the baby is asleep fast.

2 The pub sign swung as it creaked in the wind.

3 I have right my books in the room on the left.

4 We are buying our car and selling a new one.

5 Please put the rail back on the towel.

Change one word so that the sentence makes sense. Underline the word you are taking out and write your new word on the line.

Example I waited in line to buy a <u>book</u> to see the film. _____*ticket*_____

6 As it is raining, we will stay outside and keep dry. _____

7 Fish are able to breathe out of water. _____

8 Tears poured down her face as she was so happy. _____

9 The dog mooed happily when she saw her calf. _____

10 Lara fell up and cut her knee. _____

Solve each question by working out the code.

11 If the code for CHOIR is ~ # £ @ *, what is the
code for RICH? _____

12 If the code for BASIN is GHYWC, what is the
code for BINS? _____

13 If the code for TIGHT is 57935, what is the
code for HIGH? _____

14 If the code for TRAIN is c b s l d , what is b s d c ? _____

15 If the code for FLOWN is − = + × > what is × + + = ? _____

Total

Answers

TEST 1: Similars and Opposites

1 story, tale
2 sight, vision
3 free, release
4 dish, bowl
5 finish, halt
6 sensible, foolish
7 war, peace
8 heavy, light
9 rise, fall
10 major, minor
11 fib
12 capture
13 lady
14 blend
15 attack

TEST 2: Sorting Words

1 FIREWORK
2 SUNDAY
3 MOVING
4 QUIET
5 PICTURE
6 A
7 B
8 B
9 A
10 B
11 simple easy
12 horse wood
13 clock sea
14 brown black
15 tiny little

TEST 3: Selecting Letters

1 e
2 b
3 f
4 z
5 e
6 bust
7 long
8 frail
9 paint
10 float
11 win
12 heat
13 cane
14 beach
15 light

TEST 4: Selecting Words

1 forehead
2 chatterbox
3 highlight
4 mushroom
5 upset
6 night, bed, teeth
7 coat, blue, red
8 hungry, dog, bone
9 rusty, gate, squeaked
10 rained, deep, playground
11 water
12 grass
13 face
14 tarmac
15 sides

TEST 5: Finding Words

1 ALL
2 RAN
3 TEA
4 DEN
5 WIN
6 seat
7 them
8 wear
9 term
10 germ
11 snail
12 state
13 thief
14 crawl
15 trees

TEST 6: Alphabetical Order and Substitution

1 brown
2 chest
3 August
4 abbot
5 bossy
6 ghost
7 glory
8 added
9 faced
10 bead
11 20
12 10
13 19
14 4
15 22

TEST 7: Word Progressions

1 STIR
2 PASS
3 MORE
4 FIRE
5 TIRE
6 CASE
7 FIRM
8 cure
9 gong
10 hit
11 sewn
12 9
13 3
14 10
15 9

TEST 8: Logic

1 Billie
2 no
3 jeans
4 10:25
5 10:50
6 6
7 15
8 12
9 Pete
10 Lewis
11 1 hr 30 mins
12 11:30
13 11:50
14 Friday
15 Sunday

TEST 9: Codes

1 ZKMH
2 HMP
3 ZHKP
4 BARE
5 WEAR
6 4613
7 9674
8 7619
9 6749
10 1993
11 2169
12 FOVD
13 YPRX
14 PINT
15 MEET

TEST 10: Sequences

1 slow, clean
2 head, hand
3 six, ten
4 throw, fall
5 depart, little
6 DB
7 10d
8 MNP
9 Q4R
10 NO
11 FV
12 AC
13 19
14 12
15 2

TEST 11: Mixed

1 DENTIST
2 FOOTBALL
3 SUMMER
4 PLAYING
5 PELICAN
6 salty, sweet
7 flexible, rigid
8 fail, pass
9 sensible, foolish
10 to, from
11 PDRL
12 3270
13 VMCF
14 GRIT
15 TALL

TEST 12: Mixed

1 w
2 e
3 r
4 g
5 d
6 15
7 33
8 24
9 444
10 14
11 most
12 foot
13 know
14 adder
15 flop

TEST 13: Mixed

1 waves, boat
2 sleepy, tired
3 wearing, not
4 storm, thunder
5 meal, mother
6 close, open
7 fast, slowly
8 carrots, letters
9 early, late
10 shorter, longer
11 warm
12 safety
13 descend
14 slight
15 arrive

TEST 14: Mixed

1 with
2 stale
3 often
4 armful
5 other
6 them
7 keys
8 scan
9 leaf
10 hare
11 ZFPW
12 PBFP
13 WFZW
14 COAT
15 TROT

TEST 15: Mixed

1 saving
2 pocket
3 bicycle
4 touch
5 bite
6 20
7 40
8 45
9 15
10 £4.70
11 £5.20
12 internet
13 suitable
14 sailor
15 behind

TEST 16: Mixed

1 wet, dry
2 hard, soft
3 shiny, dull
4 multiply, divide
5 find, conceal
6 B
7 A
8 A
9 B
10 A
11 RQ
12 aO
13 7C
14 6V
15 QS

TEST 17: Mixed

1 c
2 a
3 c
4 b
5 a

10 tiny, mouse, tall
11 scaly, tail, breathe
12 away, books, out
13 walk, swings, play
14 lunch, sausages, salad
15 tattered, scarecrow, field

TEST 18: Mixed

1 21
2 80
3 8.5
4 4M4
5 20
6 fall
7 prick
8 pour
9 stream
10 pray
11 world
12 rabbit
13 tunnels
14 Friday
15 classical

TEST 19: Mixed

1 coats
2 outside
3 right
4 straight
5 street
6 slow, low
7 choose, rise
8 rough, stormy
9 Tuesday, Sunday
10 dog, horse
11 5761
12 1657
13 1697
14 7931
15 SPORT

TEST 20: Mixed

1 hide
2 gloomy
3 absent
4 unsafe
5 plain
6 OWE
7 PET
8 TEA
9 AND
10 TOO
11 nose
12 walls
13 trees
14 sides
15 a sole

TEST 21: Mixed

1 staff
2 pain
3 laid
4 what
5 stale
6 beetle, wasp
7 some, few
8 sum, metre
9 line, row
10 happy, laugh
11 HG
12 YZA
13 ef34
14 9WX
15 ACC

TEST 22: Mixed

1 hand
2 wind
3 work
4 butter
5 high
6 E
7 F
8 C
9 D
10 B
11 A

12

G	O	O	D
A	■	N	■
M	A	L	E
E	■	Y	■

14

B	A	T	H
■	O	■	U
O	W	L	S
■	K	■	H

13

A	■	■	H
G	A	L	A
E	■	■	Z
S	A	F	E

15

■	T	■	J
Z	U	L	U
■	R	■	M
S	N	I	P

TEST 23: Mixed

1 asleep, fast
2 swung, creaked
3 right, left
4 buying, selling
5 rail, towel
6 outside, inside
7 able, unable
8 happy, sad
9 dog, cow
10 up, down
11 * @ ~ #
12 GWCY
13 3793
14 RANT
15 WOOL

TEST 24: Mixed

1 lie, truth
2 backwards, forwards
3 dawn, dusk
4 broad, narrow
5 far, near
6 8
7 12
8 20
9 t
10 t
11 chief
12 labelled
13 decide
14 dabble
15 jackal

TEST 25: Mixed

1 LAP, PAL
2 DRAW, WARD
3 APT, TAP
4 LEFT, FELT
5 BEARD, BREAD
6 BEAR
7 POOR
8 PIES
9 WIDE
10 HAZY
11 outside, under
12 large, little
13 head, finger
14 pen, brush
15 firm, smooth

Test 26: Mixed

1 peculiar
2 annoy
3 direct
4 glance
5 pour
6 four
7 wine
8 hate
9 nest
10 they
11 tank
12 angle
13 swam
14 sight
15 step

Test 27: Mixed

1 MINE
2 SLOT
3 BASH
4 LUNG
5 BEAT
6 garden, letter
7 oval, circle
8 one, two
9 money, shop
10 dark, tough
11 12
12 1
13 11
14 9
15 2

Test 28: Mixed

1 VX
2 13G
3 CB
4 G4H
5 wxy
6 f
7 b
8 n
9 e
10 c
11 lift, raise
12 wander, stray
13 weird, odd
14 furry, hairy
15 fight, battle

Test 29: Mixed

1 HPQJ
2 CPQH
3 QXHR
4 QPHZ
5 BALL
6 peel, skin
7 reply, respond
8 giggle, chuckle
9 gather, assemble
10 entire, complete
11 boring
12 bush
13 wolf
14 from
15 star

Test 30: Mixed

1 19
2 17
3 12
4 20
5 3
6 THE
7 ARC
8 HUT
9 ASH
10 AIR
11 tent
12 wasp
13 first
14 plain
15 steep

Test 31: Mixed

1 5493
2 2745
3 2453
4 TEAM
5 MATE
6 legs
7 a mattress
8 pages
9 wheels
10 food
11 PILE
12 FLAP
13 WADE
14 FOOL
15 MICE

Test 32: Mixed

1 h
2 t
3 o
4 w
5 k
6 tour
7 vest
8 card
9 dove
10 than
11 grin
12 blade
13 nose
14 drain
15 roast

Test 33: Mixed

5 2
6 art
7 Friday
8 Child C
9 Child B
10 Child C
11 chew, chat
12 month, day
13 peace, happiness
14 cushion, mat
15 4 legs, 2 legs

Test 34: Mixed

1 11
2 75
3 8
4 9
5 10y
6 Leeds, London
7 left, dark
8 cloud, basin
9 mirror, picture
10 daughter, mother
11 nervous
12 chief
13 beneath
14 changeable
15 burn

Test 35: Mixed

1 APE, PEA
2 LAIR, RAIL
3 REAR, RARE
4 ITS, SIT
5 TASTE, STATE

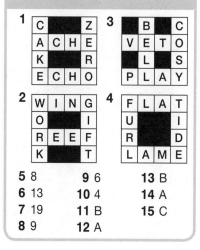

10 controlled, passed, goal
11 listen, instructions, shouted
12 that, iceberg, water
13 sheep, horns, not
14 finished, writing, play
15 school, learning, life

Test 36: Mixed

1 OWN
2 YES
3 RAN
4 OUR
5 TEN
6 cats
7 dogs
8 5
9 others
10 fish
11 20
12 bathroom
13 bitten
14 knowledge
15 quicksand

Test 37: Mixed

5 8
6 13
7 19
8 9
9 6
10 4
11 B
12 A
13 B
14 A
15 C

TEST 38: Mixed

1 h	**8** tint, hue
2 p	**9** knot, fasten
3 d	**10** smooth, silky
4 s	**11** talk
5 k	**12** low
6 breadth, width	**13** sandwich
	14 screw
7 save, conserve	**15** night

TEST 39: Mixed

1 13	**6** hour	**11** sneer
2 3	**7** stop	**12** treat
3 28	**8** land	**13** stand
4 44	**9** seal	**14** slide
5 20	**10** fern	**15** swoon

TEST 40: Mixed

1 LAKE	**6** SON	**11** VX
2 FURL	**7** BOW	**12** 2DX
3 PACK	**8** OUT	**13** JIL
4 BEAT	**9** ATE	**14** ghi
5 FOOL	**10** CAR	**15** 9AC

Puzzle ❶

Puzzle ❷

wand	kill	reel
dart	laid	loaf
trip	down	flip
park	near	prow

Puzzle ❸

1 angle		**7** straw
2 ropes		**8** peach
3 broad		**9** state
4 cheat		**10** table
5 spear		**11** worth
6 gable		**12** stale

Puzzle ❹

W	EAR	AIL	TOP	HIP	ASH
	BID	HEN	ALL	ARM	KIT
S	OAK	JAR	CAN	TAR	CAR
	WAN	TOW	PIT	ALL	OWL
F	ATE	ILL	AIR	ITS	OUR
	OAR	ICE	ASH	FOX	MOW
R	EEL	HOP	AIL	ATE	EAR
	OAR	ICE	ASH	SEA	MOW

Puzzle ❺

1 February
2 December

Underline the two words, one from each group, which are the most opposite in meaning.

Example   (dawn, <u>early</u>, wake) (<u>late</u>, stop, sunrise)

1 (sleep, lie, work)   (night, snore, truth)

2 (backwards, down, beside)   (forwards, inside, across)

3 (moon, light, dawn)   (day, dusk, night)

4 (talk, broad, tall)   (chatter, wide, narrow)

5 (far, steady, closed)   (distant, near, firm)

If q = 2, r = 3, s = 5 and t = 10, find the value of:

6 $(r + t) - s =$ _____

7 $6q =$ _____

8 $q + r + s + t =$ _____

Now give the answers of these calculations as letters:

9 $sq =$ _____

10 $q + r + s =$ _____

Underline the word in each line which uses only letters from the first 12 letters of the alphabet. The alphabet has been written out to help you.

A B C D E F G H I J K L M N O P Q R S T U V W X Y Z

11	basket	lettuce	flannel	chief
12	labelled	bridge	chimney	fussy
13	dragon	decide	flavour	current
14	bitten	joker	dabble	laugh
15	lantern	casket	jackal	height

Time for a break! Go to Puzzle Page 41 ▶

Total ___

Underline the two words which are made from the same letters.

Example	TAP	PET	<u>TEA</u>	POT	<u>EAT</u>

1	LAP	PAW	PAL	SAP	SAW
2	CARD	DRAW	CROW	WARD	WORD
3	FAT	TAR	FAR	APT	TAP
4	LEFT	FLED	FELT	FEED	DEFT
5	DREAD	BEARD	TREAT	TRADE	BREAD

Look at the first group of three words. The word in the middle has been made from the other two words. Complete the second group of three words in the same way, making a new word in the middle.

Example	PAIN	INTO	<u>TOO</u>K	ALSO	<u>SOON</u>	ONLY

6	DENT	DESK	SKIP	BEAN	_____	ARCH
7	FELT	FOOT	BOOK	PEAR	_____	SOOT
8	LIFE	LIPS	TAPS	PILE	_____	EYES
9	GIFT	GIVE	VEST	WISH	_____	DEFY
10	MILK	MOON	SOON	HIGH	_____	LAZY

Complete the following sentences in the best way by choosing one word from each set of brackets.

Example   Tall is to (tree, <u>short</u>, colour) as narrow is to (thin, white, <u>wide</u>).

11   Inside is to (house, garden, outside) as over is to (above, under, near).

12   Big is to (elephant, large, tiny) as small is to (little, pain, quick).

13   Hair is to (head, ribbon, long) as nail is to (wood, hammer, finger).

14   Ink is to (pencil, word, pen) as paint is to (brush, colour, red).

15   Slippery is to (eel, firm, mud) as bumpy is to (smooth, road, track).

Total

TEST 26: **Mixed**

Underline the word in the brackets closest in meaning to the word in capitals.

Example   UNHAPPY   (unkind   death   laughter   <u>sad</u>   friendly)

1   STRANGE   (ordinary   usual   extra   visitor   peculiar)

2   VEX   (tired   annoy   please   wonder   chew)

3   STRAIGHT   (curved   narrow   direct   lined   crooked)

4   PEEP   (peck   glide   stare   horn   glance)

5   TIP   (pour   catch   money   bottom   bin)

Find the four-letter word hidden at the end of one word and the beginning of the next word. The order of the letters may not be changed.

Example   The children had ba<u>ts and</u> balls.   _____sand_____

6   Please take those coats off our chairs.   _____

7   Ravi is so quick, he will win every race.   _____

8   Sarah ate a whole tin of toffees.   _____

9   One star is shining particularly brightly.   _____

10   Leaves are blowing in the air in the yard.   _____

Remove one letter from the word in capitals to leave a new word. The meaning of the new word is given in the clue.

Example   AUNT   an insect   _____ant_____

11   THANK   container   _____

12   TANGLE   corner   _____

13   SWARM   bathed   _____

14   SLIGHT   vision   _____

15   STEEP   tread   _____

Total

Change the first word into the last word, by changing one letter at a time and making a new, different word in the middle.

Example	CASE	_CASH_	LASH

1   WINE   _____   MINT

2   SLIT   _____   SLOW

3   WASH   _____   BATH

4   RUNG   _____   LONG

5   BEST   _____   BOAT

Underline the two words which are the odd ones out in the following groups of words.

Example   black   <u>king</u>   purple   green   <u>house</u>

6   respect   garden   value   prize   letter

7   square   rectangle   hexagon   oval   circle

8   one   two   third   fourth   fifth

9   cost   expense   money   shop   price

10   dark   light   flimsy   delicate   tough

Find the missing number by using the two numbers outside the brackets in the same way as the other sets of numbers.

Example   2 [8] 4   3 [18] 6   5 [25] 5

11   16 [14] 2   24 [12] 12   18 [___] 6

12   20 [5] 4   10 [2] 5   8 [___] 8

13   3 [7] 4   5 [13] 8   4 [___] 7

14   5 [25] 5   4 [16] 4   3 [___] 3

15   8 [2] 4   12 [3] 4   12 [___] 6

Total

Test time: 0 | | | | | 5 | | | | 10 minutes

Fill in the missing letters and numbers.
The alphabet has been written out to help you.

A B C D E F G H I J K L M N O P Q R S T U V W X Y Z

Example   AB is to CD as PQ is to _RS_.

1   MO is to PR as SU is to _____.

2   19D is to 17E as 15F is to _____.

3   ML is to KJ as ED is to _____.

4   A1B is to C2D as E3F is to _____.

5   nop is to qrs as tuv is to _____.

Which one letter can be added to the front of all these words to make new words?

Example   _C_ are   _C_ at   _C_ rate   _C_ all

6   ___ arm   ___ attest   ___ ox   ___ ling

7   ___ rain   ___ right   ___ last   ___ lank

8   ___ ape   ___ ought   ___ ail   ___ ice

9   ___ ager   ___ mpty   ___ at   ___ yes

10   ___ limb   ___ rust   ___ rash   ___ lock

Underline the two words, one from each group, that are closest in meaning.

Example   (race, shop, <u>start</u>)   (finish, <u>begin</u>, end)

11   (lift, choose, cling)   (raise, drop, fall)

12   (know, path, wander)   (wonder, stray, run)

13   (few, weird, even)   (normal, odd, many)

14   (furry, hairless, muddy)   (clean, tiny, hairy)

15   (sight, fight, might)   (battle, hearing, claim)

29

Total

Test 29: **Mixed**

These words have been written in code but the codes are not under the correct words. Match each word to the correct code.

MILK	FILM	LAMB	LIMP
QXHR	QPHZ	CPQH	HPQJ

1 MILK _____

2 FILM _____

3 LAMB _____

4 LIMP _____

Using the same code, decode:

5 RXQQ _____

Underline the pair of words most similar in meaning.

Example   come, go   <u>roam, wander</u>   fear, fare

6	pick, mix	forgive, forget	peel, skin
7	reply, respond	question, answer	ask, shout
8	laugh, cry	weeping, smiling	giggle, chuckle
9	collect, deliver	take, away	gather, assemble
10	entrance, exit	entire, complete	play, ground

Change the first word of the third pair in the same way as the other pairs to give a new word.

Example   bind, hind   bare, hare   but, _____hut_____

11	comb, coming	town, towing	bore, _____
12	rust, rush	crust, crush	bust, _____
13	nuts, stun	drab, bard	flow, _____
14	loin, lion	silt, slit	form, _____
15	pillow, pill	milked, milk	starts, _____

Total

If v = 3, w = 8, y = 5 and z = 7, find the value of:

1 vw – y = _____

2 2y + z = _____

3 3z – 3v = _____

4 w + y + z = _____

5 w – y = _____

Find the three-letter word which can be added to the letters in capitals to make a new word. The new word will complete the sentence sensibly.

Example The cat sprang onto the MO.   _USE_

6 Put them on the table over RE please.   _____

7 Simon is the postman who delivers letters and PELS in our street.   _____

8 Our teacher likes us to S the door quietly, not slam it.   _____

9 The children SPLED merrily in the puddles.   _____

10 The old man sits in his favourite ARMCH by the fire.   _____

Add one letter to the word given in capital letters to make a new word. The meaning of the new word is given in the clue.

Example PLAN   simple   _plain_

11 TEN   a cloth shelter   _____

12 WAS   an insect   _____

13 FIST   before second   _____

14 PLAN   not patterned   _____

15 STEP   high and sloping   _____

Total [   ]

Test time: 0 | | | | | 5 | | | | | 10 minutes

If the code for MARKET is 547932, what are the codes for the following words?

1 MAKE   _____

2 TRAM   _____

3 TAME   _____

Using the same code, decode:

4 2345   _____

5 5423   _____

Choose the word or phrase that makes each sentence true.

Example   A LIBRARY always has (posters, carpets, <u>books</u>, DVDs, stairs).

6 A BEETLE always has (legs, stripes, food, shelter, spots).

7 A BED always has (a duvet, pillows, pyjamas, a mattress, sheets).

8 A BOOK always has (a story, pictures, a bookshelf, a library, pages).

9 A CAR always has (a driver, passengers, a boot, wheels, four doors).

10 A GROCERY SHOP always has (a restaurant, clothes, food, flowers, a bakery).

Look at the first group of three words. The word in the middle has been made from the other two words. Complete the second group of three words in the same way, making a new word in the middle.

Example   PA<u>IN</u>   <u>IN</u>TO   <u>TO</u>OK   ALSO   __*SOON*__   ONLY

11	BELT	BEAN	ANTS	PICK	_____	LEAN
12	QUIP	QUAY	BRAY	FLEW	_____	SWAP
13	JAMS	JOIN	COIN	WEST	_____	FADE
14	SPUN	SOON	WOOL	FAIL	_____	TOOK
15	KING	KILT	SALT	MILK	_____	FACE

Total _____

Test time: 0 ‖‖‖‖‖‖‖‖‖‖ 5 ‖‖‖‖‖ 10 minutes

Find the letter which will end the first word and start the second word.

Example peac (_h_) ome

1 pat (____) ope

2 bel (____) han

3 her (____) nce

4 cla (____) ise

5 bac (____) ite

Find the four-letter word hidden at the end of one word and the beginning of the next word. The order of the letters may not be changed.

Example The children had ba<u>ts and</u> balls. ___sand___

6 All of us caught our balls. _____

7 The waves tossed the boat. _____

8 The old car door was very rusty. _____

9 The horse jumped over the fence. _____

10 Both animals were extremely fierce. _____

Underline the one word which **cannot be made** from the letters of the word in capital letters.

Example	STATIONERY	stones	tyres	ration	<u>nation</u>	noisy
11	THINKING	grin	king	thin	ink	hint
12	BATTLES	slate	bats	steal	blade	bleat
13	CUSHION	such	nose	coin	shun	chin
14	BIRTHDAY	dirt	yard	drab	bath	drain
15	HISTORY	story	shirt	roast	hoist	rosy

33

Time for a break! Go to Puzzle Page 42

Total _____

Fill in the crosswords so that all the given words are included.
You have been given one letter as a clue in each crossword.

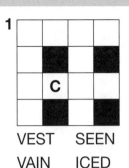

1

VEST   SEEN
VAIN   ICED

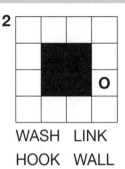

2

WASH LINK
HOOK WALL

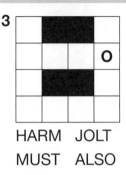

3

HARM JOLT
MUST ALSO

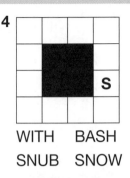

4

WITH BASH
SNUB SNOW

Some children have after school activities.

Child A has ballet on Monday, dancing on Thursday and tennis on Saturday.
Child B has scouts on Wednesday and football on Sunday. Child C has ballet
on Monday, art on Tuesday, music on Thursday and athletics on Saturday.
Child D has swimming on Monday, scouts on Wednesday and football on
Sunday. Child E has swimming on Monday, dancing on Thursday and tennis
on Saturday.

5   How many children play football?   _____

6   Which activity takes place on Tuesday?   _____

7   On which day is there no activity?   _____

8   Which child has the most activities?   _____

9   Which child has Mondays free but is busy on Sundays?   _____

10 Which child does activities that none of the others do?   _____

Complete the following sentences in the best way by choosing one
word from each set of brackets.

Example   Tall is to (tree, <u>short</u>, colour) as narrow is to (thin, white, <u>wide</u>).

11   Bite is to (food, swallow, chew) as talk is to (phone, eat, chat).

12   February is to (winter, month, year) as Sunday is to (weekend, day, holiday).

13   War is to (peace, battle, fight) as sadness is to (happiness, rain, darkness).

14   Pillow is to (cushion, bed, feather) as rug is to (room, picture, mat).

15   Cat is to (whiskers, tail, 4 legs) as man is to (woman, 2 legs, arms).

Total

TEST 34: **Mixed**

Fill in the missing numbers and letters in each sequence.

Example	2	4	6	8	10	_12_

1	7	____	15	19	23	27
2	31	42	53	64	____	86
3	2	4	____	16	32	64
4	21	16	12	____	7	6
5	____	13x	16w	19v	22u	25t

Underline the two words which are the odd ones out in the following groups of words.

Example	black	<u>king</u>	purple	green	<u>house</u>

6	Wales	Leeds	London	Scotland	Ireland
7	right	left	fair	honest	dark
8	candle	lamp	torch	cloud	basin
9	mirror	newspaper	book	picture	magazine
10	son	daughter	grandfather	nephew	mother

Underline the word in the brackets closest in meaning to the word in capital letters.

Example	UNHAPPY	(unkind	death	laughter	<u>sad</u>	friendly)

11	TIMID	(nervous	bold	quick	expensive	brave)
12	MAIN	(water	chief	stay	part	pony)
13	UNDER	(over	beside	beneath	inside	outside)
14	VARIABLE	(plain	constant	coloured	changeable	fixed)
15	SINGE	(tuneful	carol	warm	beat	burn)

Total

Test 35: **Mixed**

Underline the two words which are made from the same letters.

Example   TAP   PET   <u>TEA</u>   POT   <u>EAT</u>

1   RAP   APE   PAT   PEA   TAR   2   NAIL   RAIN   LAIR   HAIR   RAIL

3   REAR   RAIN   NEAR   REAL   RARE   4   NET   ITS   TIN   SIT   SET

5   TASTE   TREAT   STATE   TOAST   TEASE

Fill in the crosswords so that all the given words are included.
You have been given one letter as a clue in each crossword.

6   7   8   9

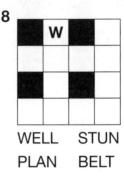
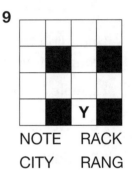

| DESK | STEW | | SOME | JAMS | | WELL | STUN | | NOTE | RACK |
| EDIT | KNOW | | JAZZ | ZOOM | | PLAN | BELT | | CITY | RANG |

Complete the following sentences by selecting the most sensible word
from each group of words given in the brackets. Underline the words selected.

Example   The (<u>children</u>, books, foxes) carried the (houses, <u>books</u>, steps)
home from the (greengrocer, <u>library</u>, factory).

10   Kieran skilfully (called, controlled, kissed) the ball and (passed, flew, pierced)
it to Darren who scored a (look, goal, pigeon).

11   'Why can't you (listen, eat, climb) carefully to (table, instructions, pebbles)?'
(shouted, dug, swam) Dad.

12   It is said (than, think, that) only one tenth of an (ice cream, icicle, iceberg) is
visible above the (fire, earth, water) surface level.

13   Some (classrooms, sheep, jackets) have (horns, waterfalls, fences) but many
do (knot, no, not).

14   When I had (started, wished, finished) (writing, eating, playing) my story, I
went out to (cry, play, work).

15   At (school, hospital, pavement) we are (learning, eating, shouting) about the
Romans and their way of (school, life, help) in Britain.

Total

TEST 36: **Mixed**

Test time: 0 .... 5 .... 10 minutes

Find the three-letter word which can be added to the letters in capitals to make a new word. The new word will complete the sentence sensibly.

Example   The cat sprang onto the MO.   <u>USE</u>

1   Please sit D on that chair.   _____

2   He has a kind face with big brown E.   _____

3   Your GDMOTHER is taller than mine.   _____

4   Driving on the motorway to London takes about half an H.   _____

5   Gina's cat has just had KITS.   _____

The chart below shows how many pets two classes have.

	DOGS	CATS	FISH	GERBILS	OTHERS	NONE
CLASS X	3	12	3	2	7	2
CLASS Y	7	9	6	0	11	3

6   Which pet is most popular of all?   _____

7   Which pet is more popular in Class Y, dogs or fish?   _____

8   How many children altogether have no pets?   _____

9   Which column has the greatest number in Class Y?   _____

10   Which pet is twice as popular in Class Y than Class X?   _____

11   How many children altogether have gerbils and 'other' pets? _____

Underline two words, one from each group, that go together to form a new word. The word in the first group always comes first.

Example   (hand, <u>green</u>, for)   (light, <u>house</u>, sure)

12   (orange, bath, bubble)   (soap, sky, room)

13   (off, soft, bit)   (ten, win, bed)

14   (know, term, win)   (rim, ledge, side)

15   (slippery, quick, stony)   (rock, change, sand)

Total

Fill in the crosswords so that all the given words are included.
You have been given one letter as a clue in each crossword.

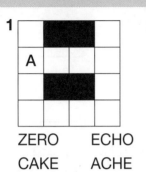

ZERO   ECHO
CAKE   ACHE

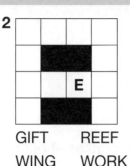

GIFT   REEF
WING   WORK

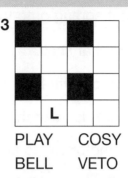

PLAY   COSY
BELL   VETO

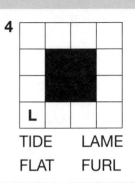

TIDE   LAME
FLAT   FURL

The houses on one side of a street are even numbers from 2 to 20.
On the other side they are odd numbers from 1 to 19.
1 is opposite 2, 3 is opposite 4 and so on.

5 What number house is opposite 7?   _____

6 What number house is opposite 14?   _____

7 What number house is a higher number and next to 17?   _____

8 Which house is a lower number and opposite to 10?   _____

House number 3 and House number 4 have blue doors.
House number 4 and House number 5 have window boxes.
House number 3 and House number 6 have large door knockers.
Houses 5 and 6 have green doors.
Which house has:

9   a green door and a large door knocker?   _____

10 a blue door and a window box?   _____

Look at these groups of words.
Group A: ON LAND   Group B: ON WATER   Group C: IN THE AIR
Choose the correct group for each of the types of transport below.
Write in the letter.

11 boat	_____	**12** train	_____
13 ship	_____	**14** van	_____
15 helicopter	_____		

Total

TEST 38: **Mixed**

Which one letter can be added to the front of all these words to make new words?

Example   _C_ are   _C_ at   _C_ rate   _C_ all

1	___ eel	___ earth	___ eat	___ and
2	___ ram	___ lease	___ ink	___ itch
3	___ evil	___ ear	___ ark	___ rink
4	___ port	___ weep	___ team	___ tray
5	___ nit	___ ill	___ not	___ night

Underline the pair of words most similar in meaning.

Example   come, go   <u>roam, wander</u>   fear, fare

6	tall, thin	high, low	breadth, width
7	look, listen	save, conserve	rash, sensible
8	tint, hue	blue, colour	sky, sea
9	tie, laces	bind, weed	knot, fasten
10	soft, touch	smooth, silky	delicate, harsh

If these words were placed in alphabetical order, which would come second to last? Underline the word.

11	talk	converse	shout	yell	call
12	high	low	below	above	up
13	biscuit	cake	sandwich	cookie	tart
14	screw	nail	tack	pin	hammer
15	light	dark	night	day	sunshine

Total

Test time: 0 | | | | | 5 | | | | | 10 minutes

Underline the number that completes each sequence.

1   21 is to 19 as 15 is to (13, 17, 11).

2   8 is to 4 as 6 is to (12, 3, 18).

3   13 is to 26 as 14 is to (27, 28, 18).

4   77 is to 66 as 55 is to (44, 555, 11).

5   1 is to 10 as 11 is to (16, 20, 2).

Find the four-letter word hidden at the end of one word and the beginning of the next word. The order of the letters may not be changed.

Example   The children had bat<u>s and</u> balls.   *sand*

6   Let's run and catch our bus.   _____

7   You must open all the windows.   _____

8   Paul and Adam liked the film too.   _____

9   Please allow enough time to get there.   _____

10   I definitely prefer nuts to raisins.   _____

Underline the one word which **cannot be made** from the letters of the word in capital letters.

Example   STATIONERY   stones   tyres   ration   <u>nation</u>   noisy

11	CORNERS	crone	rose	snore	sneer	corn
12	FEATHER	there	reef	treat	fear	heart
13	DUSTING	stand	gust	stud	sting	sung
14	SEASIDE	seed	slide	aside	dies	ease
15	WOODLAND	wool	load	wand	lawn	swoon

Total

TEST 40: **Mixed**

Change the first word into the last word, by changing one letter at a time and making a new, different word in the middle.

| Example | CASE | _CASH_ | LASH |

1	WAKE	_____	LAME
2	HURL	_____	FURY
3	PICK	_____	BACK
4	FEAT	_____	BOAT
5	TOOL	_____	FOAL

Find the three-letter word which can be added to the letters in capitals to make a new word. The new word will complete the sentence sensibly.

| Example | The cat sprang onto the MO. | _USE_ |

6   In our Music LES today, we played guitars.   _____

7   Look at the beautiful RAIN arching across the sky!   _____

8   Talking very loudly is called SHING.   _____

9   In the countryside you must close GS to fields behind you. _____

10 Mrs Newman has a new PET in her sitting room.   _____

Give the missing groups of letters and numbers in the following sequences. The alphabet has been written out to help you.

A B C D E F G H I J K L M N O P Q R S T U V W X Y Z

Example	CQ	DP	EQ	FP	GQ	_HP_
11	BD	FH	JL	NP	RT	___
12	2AX	2BX	2CX	___	2EX	2FX
13	BAD	FEH	___	NMP	RQT	VUX
14	abc	DEF	___	JKL	mno	PQR
15	___	8EG	7IK	6MO	5QS	4UW

Time for a break! Go to Puzzle Page 42 ▶

Total [   ]

Puzzle

Noughts and Crosses

NORTH

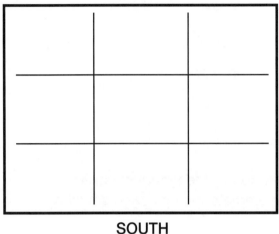

SOUTH

Follow the instructions using the compass points, and place the Os and ✗s in the correct places. Draw a line to show who wins the game by getting three of their symbols in a row.

1 ✗ in the NW box.

2 O in the SE box.

3 ✗ in the SW box.

4 O in the W box.

5 ✗ in the NE box.

6 O in the centre.

7 ✗ in the N box.

Puzzle 2

Clock Words

Here is an unusual clock! Each of the numbers has been replaced by a letter.

Start at '12 o'clock' and go round the letters making words back up to the w at the top.

As you work your way round the clock, each missing word begins and ends with one of the letters in the squares. The missing words are shown in the body of the clock. The first one has been done for you.

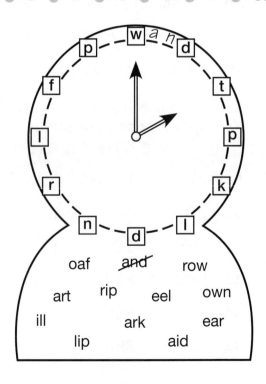

oaf   and   row

art   rip   eel   own

ill   ark   ear

lip   aid

Puzzle ③

Arranging Anagrams

The letters of the following words can be rearranged to make different words.

There are 3 sections to this puzzle. First try to solve the anagram by looking at Section 1. To check your answer, look at the clues in Section 2. If you still can't solve it, in Section 3 you will find the word in a mixed list.

SECTION 1		
1	angel	_angle_
2	spore	
3	board	
4	teach	
5	reaps	
6	bagel	
7	warts	
8	cheap	
9	taste	
10	bleat	
11	throw	
12	least	

SECTION 2	
1	a corner
2	cords, bonds
3	wide, not narrow
4	to swindle
5	a weapon you throw
6	the end of a building
7	animal bedding
8	a juicy fruit
9	USA is divided into 50 of these
10	you eat on it, sitting on a chair
11	value
12	not fresh

SECTION 3			
~~angle~~	gable	ropes	spear
table	straw	state	peach
cheat	worth	stale	broad

Puzzle ④

Word Wall

Shade the bricks that make a word that starts with the letter in bold. Each letter in bold uses two bars. Here is an example.

B	OLD	ASH	FIN	OWN
	ARM	ALL	EAR	END

W	EAR	AIL	TOP	HIP	ASH
	BID	HEN	ALL	ARM	KIT
S	OAK	JAR	CAN	TAR	CAR
	WAN	TOW	PIT	ALL	OWL
F	ATE	ILL	AIR	ITS	OUR
	OAR	ICE	ASH	FOX	MOW
R	EEL	HOP	AIL	ATE	EAR
	OAR	ICE	ASH	SEA	MOW

Puzzle ⑤

Alphabet Scramble

Put the letters of each of these words into alphabetical order.

1

CHIEF	_____	SQUIRT	_____
BABY	_____	BANANA	_____
UGLY	_____	BETTER	_____
ZANY	_____	STAIR	_____

2

DANGER	_____	BADGE	_____
BABBLE	_____	PORTS	_____
SUMMER	_____	ESCAPE	_____
BACON	_____	EAGLES	_____

Now take the third letter of each of your new nonsense words and rearrange them to spell out two months of the year.

1 _____   2 _____

Progress Grid

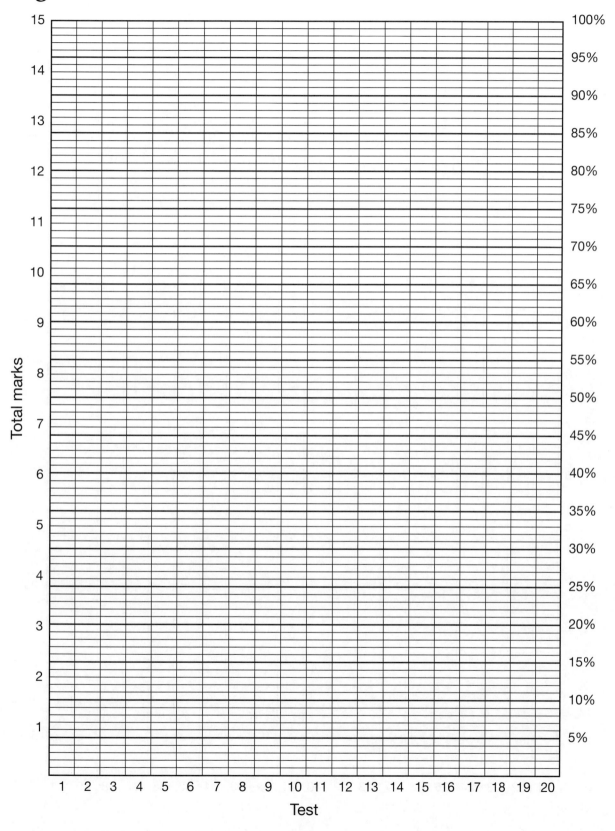

Progress Grid

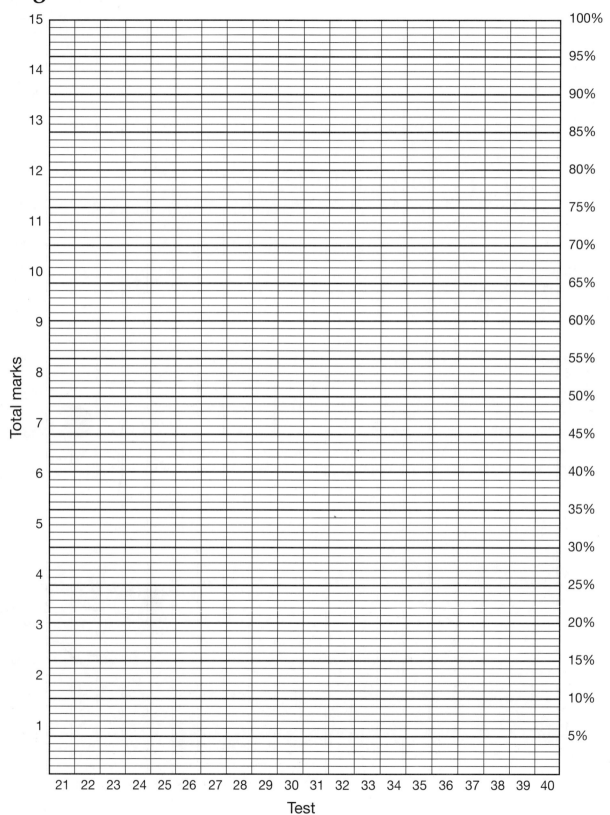

Total marks

Test